Mastering Essential Stitches and Patterns

Your Comprehensive Guide to Starting Your Crochet Journey

Bridget B Lindsay

TABLE OF CONTENTS

Crochet Stitches
Beginners Guide

CHAPTER 1: BASIC STITCHES

This section is designed to give you some of the most basic crochet stitches that are very beginner friendly. You can use these stitches for entire projects or the basis of these stitches as a frame for more advanced stitches found later in this guide.

SINGLE CROCHET

When learning how to crochet, single crochet will become your best friend. It is the core stitch you will need to learn because it is incorporated into many crochet patterns you will come across. The single crochet has the appearance of a very tight piece of fabric. It has very few holes in it and has distinctive uniform rows that look elegant and crisp. This gives your work a very clean look. Height wise, single crochet is one of the smallest of the crochet stitches; therefore work tends to build slowly when using this stitch.

To single crochet begin with your chain or row, insert your crochet hook into the next stitch or chain along. Put your yarn over your hook and draw that yarn through the hole, once you have brought the yarn through the stitch or chain you should now have 2 loops on your hook. Yarn over again and draw that yarn through both of these loops on your hook. You should now be left with only 1 loop on your hook, and that is it! That is how simple a single crochet is.

SLIP STITCH

A slip stitch, like the single crochet, is one of the basics. It has a huge variety of uses and is crucial to learn early. A row of slip stitches looks very uniform and tight. This stitch is not typically used for large sheets of fabric or objects due to how tightness of the stitches. The most common use for this stitch is for crossing a row without adding any more height to your work. It is also used to make something tighter, such as the rim of a hat. Slip stitches are commonly used to join two bits of work together such as two sheets of fabric; to do this you work a slip stitch through both pieces of fabric to join them together.

To slip stitch insert your crochet hook into the next stitch along, yarn over and draw this yarn from back to front through the stitch, now bring that yarn through the loop that is already on your hook, and that is it! This can be a little fiddly to get the hang of, but you can make it easier by making the loop on your hook a little looser, this helps with pulling the yarn through the loop.

DOUBLE CROCHET

A double crochet is twice the height of a single crochet and is just as easy. This crochet stitch has a much more open look and projects using this stitch will build very quickly. Due to the height of this stitch you will tend to need a larger starting chain; otherwise your work can begin to look warped.

To double crochet, begin by yarning over your hook, this will leave you with 2 loops on your hook. Insert the crochet hook into the next stitch (or 3rd stitch if starting at the beginning of a row) and yarn over once more and draw that yarn through the stitch. You will now have 3 loops on your hook. Yarn over once again and draw that yarn through 2 of the 3 loops only, once this is complete you will have 2 loops left on the hook. Yarn over a final time and draw the yarn through the last 2 loops on your hook and you are done.

CHAPTER 2: ADVANCED STITCHES

This section will focus on the fiddly and more advanced crochet stitches. All of these stitches use the basic stitches reviewed in the previous section, but with slight variations. The results are unique and unusual stitches you can use in your next project.

HALF DOUBLE CROCHET

This stitch is a variant of a double crochet. The height of this stitch is hallway between single and double crochet. This stitch has fewer steps than a double crochet which makes it a favorite among many people. Another significant attribute of this stitch is that it is tall like a double crochet but has the density of a single crochet.

To make a half double crochet, begin by yarning over your hook. This will leave you with 2 loops on your hook. Insert the crochet hook into the next stitch and yarn over once more and draw that yarn through the stitch, you will now have 3 loops on your hook. At this point all of these steps are the same as a double crochet, it is how you finish the stitch that is different. Yarn over and pull that yarn through all 3 loops that are on your hook to complete the stitch, and that is it!

TREBLE CROCHET

A treble crochet is a very tall stitch. It is commonly used for large open projects such as light weight blankets. This stitch does require quite a few steps, but once you have mastered how to do this, it will not take very long at all. As with double crochet, you will need to compensate when turning your work by chaining 3-5 depending on the pattern.

To begin yarn over 2 times, you should start with 3 loops on your hook. Insert your hook into the stitch, yarn over and pull the yarn through the stitch giving you 4 loops on the hook. Yarn over and pull through 2 of the 4 loops on your hook, you will be left with 3 loops after pulling through. Yarn over again and pull through another 2 loops; you will be left with 2 loops on your hook. Yarn over a final time and pull through the remaining 2 loops on your hook. Yes, it is a bit time-consuming and tricky to work with, but the results are worth it.

A great way to remember how many times to pull through the loops is in the names, a single crochet only pulls through the loops once; a double crochet pulls through the loops twice, and the treble crochet will pull through the loops three times.

FRONT POST DOUBLE CROCHET

The front post double crochet can be tricky to learn, especially if you are new to crochet. The confusion comes from the placement of your hook. The front post double crochet is simply a regular double crochet, but what makes it unique is where you will place your hook before beginning this stitch.

The finished stitch will give you the effect of a raised edge or ridge through your work. When used in conjunction with a back post double crochet, it can create a beautiful pattern.

To begin do a standard row of double crochet, this is your foundation for this stitch. If the foundation is not done, the stitch will not work. Chain 2 when you reach the end of this row.

At the beginning of your new row, yarn over and instead of inserting your hook into the top of the double crochet stitch, go under and around the stitch or post itself as shown.

Now yarn over and pull the yarn through the way you came. Finish off with a regular double crochet by yarning over and going through 2 loops, yarning over and going through the final 2 loops.

BACK POST DOUBLE CROCHET

Like the front post double crochet, this is simply a glorified double crochet, but put into a different place to create a unique little design in your work. This stitch can be used by itself or in conjunction with the front post double crochet to create a fun raised and sunken texture within your projects.

To begin, do a regular row of double crochet to form the foundation for this stitch Chain 2 at the end of your row for turning.

Now yarn over and instead of going into the top of the stitch, go behind your work and insert your hook around the post of the stitch as shown. From this position yarn over and pull the yarn through the path which you came to draw up a loop. Once you have your 3 loops on the hook, yarn over and draw through 2 loops. Yarn over and pull through the final 2 loops just like in a regular double crochet.

The front and back post double crochet work very well together and can create a type of stitch known as a basket weave, covered later on in this guide. These two stitches are also a perfect example of how you can take a regular basic stitch like the double crochet and alter it slightly to give you a great effect.

CHAPTER 3: TEXTURED STITCHES

This section will focus on textured stitches. There are a wide variety of crochet stitches that give great textures through fairly simple methods; this has been a reason crochet has become so popular. The stitches in this section are relatively easy to complete, and some of them are just an expansion of stitches taught in previous sections of this book.

FRONT LOOP CROCHET

Not to be confused with the similar front post crochet, this stitch is simple and doesn't have much of an impact. The stitch can make your plain objects have a touch of pizazz with no extra effort; as it utilizes a very basic and user-friendly single crochet.

To begin, first you need to see where your crochet hook goes. You can see from the top view of a chain or row of single crochet that you have two distinctive loops. For a regular crochet you would use both of these loops when inserting your hook, however for a front loop crochet you will be going through that first loop closest to you only!

Once at this stage simply yarn over and pull through. Yarn over and go through both 2 loops on your hook exactly like you would in a double crochet, there is nothing more to this stitch, but to make more of them!

BACK LOOP CROCHET

Just like in the front loop crochet, do not get this stitch confused with a back post double crochet as they are 2 different things. Just like the front loop crochet, this stitch utilizes the basic single crochet to create a pattern that is unique. This particular type of crochet is also used in making items like shoes and containers, as it manipulates the yarn to bend and fold in the required directions.

To begin, first you need to see where your crochet hook goes, you can clearly see from the top view of a chain or row of single crochet that you have two distinctive loops. For a regular crochet, you would use both of these loops when inserting your hook. However, for a back loop crochet you will be inserting your hook through the back loop only. Once you have done this, yarn over as you would with a single crochet, pull the yarn through, yarn over and pull through both of the 2 loops on your hook to complete the stitch.

MOSS STITCH

The Moss stitch uses 2 different crochet stitches to add a unique look to your work. This is a simple yet intriguing stitch that will spruce up many of your projects.

-Begin at the beginning of your row, and start by putting a regular half double crochet in that first stitch, and then slip stitch into the next stitch. Repeat this pattern of one half double crochet and one slip stitch to the end of the row. You will be able to clearly see a little dip in your work wherever you did a slip stitch.

-Once you reach the end of your row, chain 1 and turn your work. Now on this row you want to do the complete opposite of the previous row, this means wherever you put a half double crochet you now want to do a slip stitch, and wherever there is a slip stitch you want to do a half double crochet.

-If you forget what stitch is where, you can look at the stitch below it. If the stitch below is small than the one next to it then it was a slip stitch, if it is taller than the stitch next to it then it was a half double crochet. Keep working this pattern until you are happy with the length of your work.

BASKET STITCH

This particular stitch makes use of the stitches covered in the advanced section of this book. It uses both the front and back post double crochet, but in a particular pattern to create a beautiful texture to any pattern.

This type of stitch is mainly used for table runners, hats and blankets. The reason is that the stitch takes a long time to complete, and the result is a dense fabric. However, you can experiment with using this stitch in any project you would like.

To begin, first start off with the correct number of chains because this pattern relies on multiples. This means you must always have enough chains in that multiple. For example, if you decide that you want 4 stitches per basket stitch then your overall number of chains should be a multiple of 4, such as 16. If you wanted 5 stitches, then it would be a multiple of 5, such as 20. For this demonstration, we will be using a multiple of 4.

-Begin by having a chain of 16 with an extra 2 for your stitch allowance. Next put one double crochet in each stitch to the end of the row, chain 2 and turn your work.

-At this stage you now want to do 4 back post double crochets, and then 4 front post double crochets, repeat this pattern to complete the row, chain 2 and turn.

-Now repeat the pattern but this time in reverse. So wherever you put a front post double crochet, put a back post double crochet and vice versa.

-Simply repeat this pattern till your work is at a length you are happy with.

X STITCH

The X stitch is a very open type of stitch. The reason it is in the textured section of this book is because it has a wonderful pattern and texture that adds a beautiful highlight to any work. The X stitch like the other stitches in this section makes use of the stitches in the basic section of this guide. Note, this particular stitch requires knowledge of the double crochet.

This stitch is worked over 2 stitches. Be sure your chain or row is an even number so you can fit all the stitches.

-To begin, skip the first stitch and put a double crochet into the second stitch. Once you complete the first double crochet, yarn over and insert the hook into the stitch or chain that you skipped previously.

-Complete this by going round the back of the first stitch, into the stitch, yarn over and pull through before finishing off like a regular double crochet.

This stitch is a little tricky to get your head around in the beginning, but it is well worth the effort as you can add a unique look to your work.

CHAPTER 4: LACE AND OPEN WORK STITCHES

This chapter will focus specifically on the crochet stitches that are open and delicate. The stitches in this section will include variations of both basic stitches and some entirely new techniques which can add a very elegant look to your work without being overly complicated.

CHAIN LACE

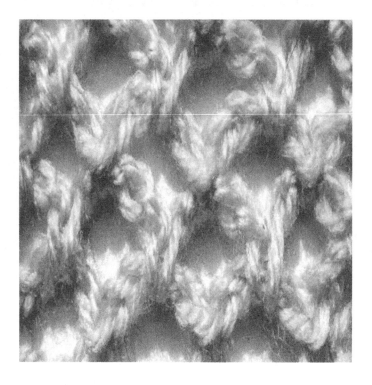

This form of lace crochet is by far one of the easiest you will come across, why? It only uses chaining to create the actual lace itself! You use one of the most basic of crocheting techniques to create this beautiful open delicate lace design to create sheets of fabric, objects or even a trim or edging.

Chain lace is worked by using multiples of 4; this means that when working chain lace you must have enough stitches in your row to be a multiple of 4 such as 16. You can however use larger multiples of 5-8 if you wanted a very open look.

-Begin by chaining your starting row of 16 (or whatever multiple you choose). Slip stitch into the 4th chain from the hook, chain another 4 and slip stitch into the 4th stitch along, repeat this once more to finish the row.

-From this point you will be working in the loops rather than individual.

-Chain 4 and slip stitch through the middle of your first loop. This can be a little difficult to see depending on how tight your work is, chain another 4 and slip stitch through the center of the next loop. Repeat this once more to finish the row.

-Repeat this series of steps to carry on with your work and simply finish off once your work has reached your desired length. Please note that this stitch can sometimes appear warped in the first few rows, this is completely normal and will even itself out as you continue.

SOLOMON'S KNOT

This stitch is commonly known as Solomon's knot; however, it is also known and can appear in patterns as the lovers knot. It is a very dainty lace design which can either be very loose or very tight depending on your preference. Solomon's knot does not use any techniques similar to that of other stitches and has its own unique method to create this type of stitch.

-To begin, start with your starting knot plus a chain 2, single crochet into the second chain from your hook. Next pull up a loop by pulling on the crochet hook, the length of this loop will determine how loose and open your Solomon's knot lace will be, the typical length for this loop is usually a maximum of half an inch.

-Now yarn over and pull the yarn through the loop, you will now have 2 bits of yarn on one side and one bit of yarn on the other side; you will need to keep these pieces separated.

-Next you will want to put your crochet hook through the center of the loop you created, pull the yarn through and perform a standard single crochet and seal it all together. Once you have completed that first knot you can repeat from the beginning by drawing up a same size loop after you finish the last single crochet and carryon from there.

V-STITCH

The crochet V stitch is the smallest stitch in this chapter. It is not considered a lace stitch, but it is a very open type of stitch hence why it is in this section. The V stitch gives any work a beautiful and delicate feel.

The V stitch is a very fast working stitch that is popular for larger projects, such as blankets and Afghans. The stitch has a great overall look and texture without being too time consuming to create.

The V stitch is worked in multiples of 7 with an extra 3 chains for turning; keep this in mind when doing your starting chain. The chain 3 you do also counts as your first double crochet of each row.

-Begin by putting a double crochet into the 4th chain from the hook, chain 1 and skip the next chain, *double crochet, chain 1, double crochet, all in the same stitch or chain then skip the next 2 chains*.

Repeat *to* to the end of the row, finish off the round with 2 double crochets in the final 2 stitches.

-In the next row start off with a double crochet, chain 1 then work *double crochet, chain 1, double crochet, all in the same stitch or chain* into every V stitch from the previous round Finish the rows off with 2 double crochets in the final 2 stitches.

That is your basic V stitch. For a more colorful effect you can switch to a different color of yarn for each row of V stitches to give it a great granny square effect to the project.

CHAPTER 5: MESH STITCHES

This section will focus on mesh stitches; this type of stitch although very open is not considered lace. The reason is that the way these stitches are laid out gives them the appearance of uniformity, such as the look of wired mesh or chicken wire. This type of stitch does not alter much in appearance, but you can change the look by increasing the height of the stitches as well as the size of the hook you use.

SMALL MESH GROUND

The small mesh ground or a single crochet mesh stitch is the smallest of the mesh stitches in this guide. This stitch makes use of the most basic of crochet techniques, the single crochet and the chain.

-To begin, on your starting chain single crochet into the 3rd chain from the hook and chain 1, skip the following chain and single crochet into the next chain, once again chain 1 and skip the next chain.

-By this point you should see a pattern forming of a tiny little grid. Do not worry if the ends look weird as they even themselves out the more of this stitch you do. Repeat the pattern of a single crochet, chain 1, skip 1, until you come to the end of your row.

-Once you reach the end of the row, chain 3 and turn your work. Next single crochet either into the top of the first single crochet you did (this lines each stitch up to make it appear more grid like) or into the chain 1 space you did (this gives your work a kind of staggered effect).

-Repeat this sequence until your work is the desired length.

LARGE MESH GROUND

The large mesh ground also called double crochet mesh stitch, just like its smaller makes use of the basic stitches of a chain stitch and a double crochet. This stitch is a lot more open than the smaller version and if completed correctly can look very delicate and pretty.

This stitch is worked in a very similar way to the smaller version except you have to allow extra stitches to compensate because a double crochet is a lot taller than a single crochet.

-To begin, start with a long chain, put one double crochet into the 5th chain from the hook, for a more basic looking mesh chain 1 and skip 1 stitch, for a more open and lace effect mesh, chain 2 and skip 2 stitches.

-Double crochet into the next chain along and chain 1-2, skip your chosen number of stitches and carry on in this fashion until you reach the end of your row. Chain 5 and turn your work, next double crochet either into the top of the first single crochet (this lines each stitch up to make it appear more grid like) or into the chain 1 space you did (this gives your work a kind of staggered effect).

-Repeat this effect until you reach the desired length.

DIAMOND MESH STITCH

This stitch is the only one in this section that does not run horizontal. The diamond mesh stitch looks very similar to chicken wire and uses the same technique as chain lace found in the lace and open work section of this guide.

The only difference between this technique and chain lace is that in chain lace you will work through the loops you create, whereas with diamond mesh you will attach each strand to a stitch making it appear more uniform and secure. You will attach your yarn to the chains using a single crochet. This gives your work a very similar appearance to the joins on a chain link fence where the wire is knotted and wrapped around each other to keep its shape.

Just like with the chain lace, you need to start with a multiple of 4 to make this work. If you wanted a larger diamond mesh then use a bigger multiple like 5 or 6, but for the purposes of the tutorial a multiple of 4 is be used.

-Begin by chaining your starting row of 20 (or any other multiple of 4), slip stitch into the 4th chain from the hook, chain another 4 and slip stitch into the 4th stitch along, repeat this once more to finish the row.

-Now, unlike with the chain lace, you will still be working into the chains rather than the loops themselves.

-Chain 4 and turn your work. You will now single crochet into the top chain of the first loop; this will either be the 2nd or 3rd chain, whichever one happens to fall at the highest point of the loop. Chain 4 and single crochet into the top chain of the next loop along, repeat this process to reach the end of the row.

-Keep in mind that just like the chain lace the beginning and ending loop of the rows may be difficult to see based on how tight you chained. Your work may also appear warped at the ends, don't worry this evens itself out the more of this stitch you do.

-Repeat these steps to grow your diamond mesh to the length you require.

CHAPTER 6: CLUSTER STITCHES

This chapter will focus on a special set of stitches called cluster stitches. These funky types of stitches create clusters by grouping large amounts of yarn together in one area. The pattern or look you get is based on the type of cluster stitch you use. Using a little amount of yarn or stitches can give you a tiny bobble, whereas using a lot of yarn or stitches in one place can give you a large puffy appearance.

PUFF STITCH

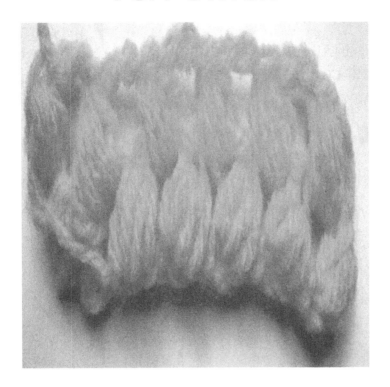

Sometimes referred to as the popcorn stitch or a bobble stitch, this is the largest and fullest of the cluster stitches in this section. It has a large puffy appearance as if it is a popped popcorn kernel. This stitch builds very slowly and does take quite a bit of yarn, but it is worth it due to the light and lovely look it gives to your projects.

-To begin chain 3 wherever it is you want to start your puff stitch. Yarn over like you would a regular double crochet and insert your hook into the next stitch along, yarn over and pull back through, you should now have 3 loops on your hook.

-Yarn over once more and insert your crochet hook into the same stitch as before, yarn over and pull up another loop. You should now have 5 loops on your hook, repeat this step 2 more times until you have a total of 9 loops on your hook (you should repeat the process 4 times to get this number).

-Now yarn over one final time and pull the yarn through all 9 loops on your hook. This can be a little tricky so take your time and go loop by loop. Once you have gone through all the loops finish with a chain 2, this stabilizes the puff stitch and stops it bending in one direction.

-To work the next puff stitch always skip one stitch to allow it enough room otherwise it can be too overcrowded.

BULLION STITCH

The bullion stitch is considered one of the hardest stitches to master. It is not only very fiddly to try to get the hang of, but there is quite a bit that can go wrong that can affect the shape of the stitch. This type of stitch is not as large as a puff stitch and can be used in every stitch or every other stitch along depending on how big you make them.

The bullion stitch itself has a unique and different appearance which can make any work you do look all the more technical. Like all cluster stitches it does take up a fair bit of yarn; but unlike the puff stitch, there are a lot less steps that go into making a bullion stitch.

-To start, begin yarning over repeatedly on your hook. The number of yarn overs you need will be specified if you are reading from a pattern. For the purposes of this tutorial, we shall yarn over a total of 4 times.

-Now insert your hook into the next stitch along, yarn over and pull through the yarn, now here comes the tricky bit! Pull that yarn through all of the yarn overs or loops you did in the beginning. This step is what gives the bullion stitch its tough reputation as you need to be able to have the right tension which takes practice to make this step work.

-Begin slowly dragging your hook and yarn through the loops you did; it can help to use a spare finger to help push the yarn overs off the hook in the beginning until you get the tension right. Once you have passed through all loops, finish off the stitch with a chain 1 to hold it all together and move on to the next stitch.

Don't worry if you do not get this straight away, this is a very hard stitch to learn and will take a fair bit of time and patience to master.

RASPBERRY STITCH

The raspberry stitch is the smallest and also the easiest of the cluster stitches within this guide. Not only does this stitch not use loops like the puff and bullion stitch, but it is also quick to do while looking just as good as the other cluster stitches.

This stitch makes use of the basic crochet stitches found within this guide including the single and double crochet. This stitch works best if you use it on top of a base of solid stitches; for example, on top of a row of single or double crochet.

-To begin, at the beginning of your row, in the first stitch put *1 single crochet, 1 double crochet, 1 single crochet* all within 1 stitch, after this skip the next 2 stitches and repeat that same sequence into the next stitch.

-And that is it! You simply repeat that sequence of stitches in a single stitch to create your raspberry stitch! It's important to note that from the front (the side you are looking at) it will not look very special. The cluster or little puff of this stitch appears on the back of your work so make sure to work inside out if you want to in the front of your projects.

CHAPTER 7: FAN AND SHELL STITCHES

This section will focus on different types of fan and shell stitches. These stitches get their name from the semi-circle or fan like appearance. Fan and shell stitches are often used to create a lovely border around projects such as blankets and Afghans. There are also lace varieties of these stitches which are popular when making lace beach cover ups or shirts.

Fan and shell stitches tend to look exactly the same and can be hard to distinguish from each other. The main difference between a fan and a shell stitch is the way they are made up. A shell stitch tends to be made up of a group of stitches in one single stitch, and a fan is usually made up in the same way but has chain spaces between each stitch making them more open. Another main difference is shell stitches will often stagger getting multiple shell stitches per row, whereas fan stitches will almost always be stacked on top of each other.

BASIC SHELL STITCH

The basic shell stitch is a very easy stitch to learn and can easily be spruced up to look like a lot of time and effort has gone into the project. A popular option with the shell stitch is to do each row in a different color, this helps to distinguish each row of shells to make them stand out. This technique is popular with the V stitch as well.

For the shell stitch, you will be working in multiples of 6 plus 1 for your turning chain.

-To begin single crochet into the second chain from the hook, skip 2 chains and put 5 double crochets into the following chain, this creates your shell. Skip the next 2 chains and single crochet into the next chain.

-Repeat this pattern of *1 single crochet, skip 2 chains, 5 double crochet into next chain, skip 2 chains, 1 single crochet in the next chain* until you reach the end of the row, chain 3 (counts as 1 double crochet) and turn your work.

-On the next row do 2 double crochet into the same area as the chain 3 you did, skip 2 double crochets from the row before and single crochet into the next one; this should be the center of the fan. Skip another 2 double crochets and do 5 double crochets into the next single crochet. Repeat this pattern to the end of the row ending with a set of 3 double crochet.

-Repeat these two steps to grow your shell stitches to the required length.

BASIC FAN STITCH

As mentioned at the beginning of this chapter, fan stitches vary from shell stitches due to the gaps in between each stitch as the fact each fan stitch will be stacked on top of one another rather than go up in a diagonal line.

This pattern only has 2 repeating rows and is worked in multiples of 8 plus 2 for your turning.

-Start with a chain of 26, single crochet into the second chain from the hook *skip 3 chains then do [1 double crochet plus a chain 1] 4 times all into one chain, do 1 more double crochet into the same shell, skip the next 3 chains and single crochet into the following chain* repeat this pattern to finish the row.

-Chain 6 and turn your work, *single crochet into the double crochet which is the center of the first fan, chain 3 and then double crochet into the next single crochet* repeat this pattern across to the end of the row.

-Chain 1 and turn your work, *skip 3 chains then do [1 double crochet plus a chain 1] 4 times all into one chain, this should line up with the top of the fan from the previous round, do 1 more double crochet into the same shell, skip the next 3 chains and single crochet into the following chain*repeat this pattern to finish the row.

-Repeat the last 2 steps to grow your work to the required length.

ARCADE STITCH

The arcade stitch is one of those stitches that have many different names and variations around the world. In some places this stitch does not even have a name. The stitch has a very distinctive open appearance that almost looks as if the fans have been reversed. Do not let the complicated look deceive you! This fan is actually remarkably easy to learn and looks fantastic at the same time!

The arcade stitch is worked using multiples of 8 plus 2 for turning.

-Start with a chain of 28, skip the first chain and single crochet into the 2nd and 3rd chain, chain 5 at this point and skip the next 5 chains and single crochet into the next 3 chains. Repeat the steps of chain 5, skip 5 chains and single crochet into the next 3 chains to finish the row, end the row with 2 single crochet rather than 3.

-Chain 1 and turn your work, do 1 single crochet into the first single crochet, skip the next stitch and work 9 double crochets into the chain 5 space from the row before* skip the first single crochet out of the set of 3 and work 1 single crochet into the second one, skip the last single crochet in the set. Work another 9 double crochet into the chain 5 space* repeat this pattern to the end of the row. Finish off by skipping one single crochet and single crocheting into the last single crochet of the row.

-Chain 4 and turn your work, skip the first 3 double crochets and single crochet into the next 3 stitches,* chain 5 and skip the next 6 double crochets, work 3 single crochets into the next 3 stitches * repeat this process across the row to the end, finish with a chain 1 and do 1 double crochet into the last stitch of the round.

-Chain 3 and work 4 double crochets in the chain 4 spaces from the previous round,* single crochet into the middle of the set of 3 single crochet, work 9 double crochet into the chain 5 space* repeat to the end of the row ending with 5 double crochets in the final gap

-Repeat all of the steps from the beginning to create and grow your arcade stitch.

CHAPTER 8: TRIMS & EDGING

So you've used all the stitches in this guide to create a beautiful piece of fabric and are wondering how exactly can you finish off the edges? This section will cover some of your options and different trims you can use to finish your work off.

PICOT EDGING

Picot edging is very dainty looking yet still makes any item look fun. A picot is a very tiny bobble made by doubling back on the work you have done; it creates cute little raised bobbles without going through the trouble of making a puff stitch.

-Begin by starting where you want your border to start from. Chain 3 from that spot, now place your hook through the 3rd chain from the hook, from here yarn over and pull the yarn through the hook. This pulls the chain down forming a little bobble.

-From this point you can either choose to make a little picot into every stitch or you can space them out a little by doing 1 or 2 single crochets in between, which creates a nice design overall.

You can work this edging all the way around the border of your projects, and it will add that extra bit of detail. If you decide to put spaces in between each picot stitch make sure that that it works out evenly to avoid getting any wrong size gaps.

REVERSE DOUBLE CROCHET EDGING

Reverse double crochet edging is another simple method of finishing. This technique is simple but adds a neat border to tidy up any wonky stitches or frayed yarn.

This particular stitch requires only a very basic stitch, the double crochet! The trick that makes this technique special is how you use it; this method can be used as a border on almost everything from blankets to booties.

-To begin, make a row of double crochet around everything you want to have a border. Make sure that if working with blankets or objects with corners to put an extra 3 double crochet in the corners to make sure your object keeps its shape.

-Next double crochet back along what you have already done but don't turn your work! This can be a little difficult to get your head around, but the effect it gives is worth it.

SHELL EDGING

The stitches used with this type of technique are very similar to that of the fans found in the fan and shell section of this guide. Note you have to make sure that when you use this finishing stitch that you have enough length on your project for the number of shells you want. If there is not enough length, you may end up with gaps in your edging work. This edging works best with either square or rectangular projects.

-Begin by doing a row of single crochet all around the project; this will form the foundation of the shells.

-Turn your work and slip stitch into the first stitch, *skip 2 stitches then put 5 double crochets into the next stitch, skip 2 more stitches and slip stitch into the following stitch*.

-Repeat this pattern again and again until you have gone all the way around; when you come to the corners, turn the corners by slip stitching round them then carrying on with the provided steps.

CHAPTER 9: SPECIAL STITCHES

This final section will focus on some of the more bizarre, less well known and difficult crochet stitches. Note that some of these stitches (especially the broomstick lace) require additional items to create them so be sure to check if the stitch you want to work requires something extra.

LOOP STITCH

The loop stitch is a funky type of stitch that adds a great amount of character to any project you use it with. The stitch itself is nothing more than a single crochet with an extra step thrown in to make the stitch possible.

The main uses of this stitch are to create hats that look like they have hair. This is a method to create the popular cabbage patch hat that has recently gained popularity. It is also a preferred stitch for baby boots and shoes.

-Start with a row of stitches of your choice; the amount does not matter as this stitch does not use sets of stitches. Begin by inserting your crochet hook through the stitch, instead of yarning over, hook around both sides of the yarn you are holding.

-Next, bring both of these pieces through the stitch, but not all the way, this should leave a small loop on the opposite side of your work. From here you can pull in the yarn you pulled through to adjust the size of the loop, yarn over and pull through all loops on your hook.

-Repeat these steps in each stitch on your work for an excellent effect!

CHEVRON STITCH

The chevron stitch, like a few stitches within this guide, makes use of basic stitches to create a beautiful effect within your work. The chevron stitch uses increases and decreases at regular intervals to make your work bend into a chevron-like pattern after just 1 row. A popular effect with this stitch is to do every row in a different color to accentuate the chevron pattern. This stitch be used on its own for an entire project or as a border for completed projects if worked correctly.

A basic full-sized chevron is worked in multiples of 14 plus an extra 2 for turning.

-Begin with your starting chain, skip the first 2 chains and double crochet into the next chain, *1 double crochet into the next 3 chains, double crochet 3 together 2 times, 1 double crochet into the next 3 chains, put 3 double crochet into the next chain twice* repeat this pattern to the end of the row ending with 3 regular double crochets.

-Chain 3 and turn your work, 2 double crochet into the first stitch, *1 double crochet in the next 3 stitches, double crochet 3 together twice, 1 double crochet in the next 3 stitches, 3 double crochet into the next stitch twice* repeat this pattern to the ending with 3 regular double crochet.

-Repeat this pattern to create your chevrons.

BROOMSTICK LACE

The broomstick lace is a type of stitch that is one of the more interesting ones available to you. The stitch itself is actually remarkably easy considering how difficult it looks.

For this stitch, you will need a regular crochet hook, regular yarn and most importantly either a broom handle (as the name suggests), a large knitting needle or anything else that is round in nature. You can also use cardboard if you do not have any of the suggested items.

-To begin, chain 21 (this will give you set of 4 broomstick lace stitches), single crochet into the 2nd chain from the hook and into every chain on your foundation, once you reach the end do not turn your work!

-Now take your broom handle or whatever you are using, for this tutorial we are using a large crochet hook. Draw up a loop and put this loop onto the second hook, take your crochet hook and insert it into the next stitch along, draw up another loop and put this on the hook, carry on in this fashion until you reach the end of the row, you should have 20 loops on the hook.

-Once the final loop is on the hook, carefully slide the loops off of the hook; make sure not to pull on the yarn to much! Now take your crochet hook and insert it through 5 loops.

-Yarn over and pull through these 5 loops and chain 1 to secure it, you now want to work 5 single crochets through the center of those 5 loops.

-Once complete go through another 5 loops and repeat the above process till you reach the end of the row, you should have 4 sets of broomstick lace at this point, instead of turning your work start drawing up loops from the single crochets you created in each 5 loop set to start the next row.

And you're done! Yes, it may look complicated, and it can get a little fiddly but the result that it gives is a great addition to your stitch knowledge!

CHAPTER 10: CONVERSION CHARTS

This section will provide you with a few charts to help you identify hook sizes and abbreviations within your work or patterns if there are terms or abbreviations you do not understand it will be here as well as a conversion chart for hook sizes.

HOOK CONVERSION CHART

Every hook size required for patterns are listed by their size in millimeters, however you may only know these hooks by the letters that they come in. Below is a handy chart showing both the numbers and letters that accompany each hook to help you identify what ones you need.

Metric Sizing – Hook Size In mm	US Standard Sizing
2.0	-
2.25	1/B
2.5	-
2.75	C
3.0	-
3.25	D
3.5	4/E
3.75	F
4.0	6/G
4.5	7
5.0	8/H
5.5	9/I
6.0	10/J
6.5	10.5/K
7.0	-
8.0	11/L
9.0	13/M
10.0	15/N

STITCH ABBREVIATIONS

Although this book does not use stitch abbreviations within the content to keep things easy to understand, when writing your own patterns or crocheting from someone else's you may come across terms you do not recognize. The chart below shows some common crochet terms in their US form.

Crochet Terminology	Abbreviation
Slip Stitch	SS or Sl St
Chain	Ch
Single Crochet	Sc
Single Crochet Two Together	sc2tog
Increasing	Inc.
Decreasing	Dec
Back Loop Only	BLO
Double Crochet	Dc
Half Double Crochet	Hdc
Repeat	Rep
Millimeter	Mm
Alternate	Alt
Treble Crochet	Tr
^^	Repeat as instructed
Continue	Cont.

Beginners Guide To Crochet Patterns

CHAPTER 1: BEGINNERS PATTERNS

This section will focus on the most basic patterns that can be done by anyone at any level. The patterns are designed to be beginner friendly and will only include basic stitches such as single and double crochet and basic increasing and decreasing.

Most of the patterns in this section can be completed within a few hours. Although simple, these patterns look fantastic.

SIMPLE BEANIE

One of the things many people struggle with when starting out with crochet is finding a decent beanie pattern that is easy to understand. Every pattern tends to have some kind of terminology or technique that you aren't familiar with so you rapidly give up on it.

Hdc....dc....sc2tog.... All of that makes no sense at the time when you are just learning the basics. I decided to come up with a design that was completely beginner friendly. I wanted it to contain only the most basic of stitches, so even someone who has just newly started could recreate this hat with a little patience. It only uses very basic beginner stitches such as chaining and slip stitches.

This pattern can be altered to look however you want. You could use funky alternating colors, maybe even add a nice flower or pin a shiny broach to it, it's all up to you!

This hat is broken down into 2 sections, the band and the hat. The band is the fitted part around your head and the hat is the main section that covers your whole head.

SUPPLIES REQUIRED

-1 ball of lightweight yarn in the color of your choice
-4mm crochet hook
-Tapestry needle
-Scissors

BAND INSTRUCTIONS

-Chain 11

-Row 1: Single crochet into the second chain from the hook and then again into the next 9 chains, chain 1 and turn (10)

-Row 2: Put one single crochet in each of the stitches across to the end of the row, chain 1 and turn (10)

-Row 3: Single crochet in each of the stitches to the end of the row, chain 1 and turn your work (10)

-Row 4-76: Single crochet in each of the stitches across to the end of the row, chain 1 and turn your work (10)

-Lay the band flat on the ground or table and bring the two ends together so that they line up> Now taking your crochet hook, slip stitch through both pieces of fabric to join them together. Make sure once you reach the end not to finish off as you will need the yarn to continue.

-Turn the band onto its side to proceed.

MAIN BEANIE INSTRUCTIONS

-Row 1: Chain 1 and then begin to place 76 single crochets around the band, you can do this however you like as long as they are evenly spaced apart. As a helpful guide it may be easier for you to place 2 single crochets into every dip in the band.

-The rest of this pattern will be worked in a continuous round. This simply means that you won't need to join or chain 1 at any point for the rest of this pattern. When you come to the end of the first round, crochet over the top of your starting point rather than join with it.

-Row 2-30: single crochet in each of the stitches in the round (76)

-Finish off leaving a long tail of yarn approximately 9-10 inches

-Next, use a tapestry needle along with the yarn you left when you finished off and begin threading the yarn through every other single crochet in your last row. Once you come back around to the beginning, gently pull on this thread to close the top of the hat. When the whole is gone, put a few simple stitches in with the needle to hold it shut.

-Weave in the ends and you're done! One finished beanie!

EASY BOW/TURBAN HEADBAND

Most crocheted headbands are a beginner's best friend. There are many different styles and types headbands available, all of which are simple to do but makes a big impact when you wear them.

Over the last few years wearing chunky headbands have really made a comeback in the fashion world especially the turban headband. This style is a regular headband with a section at the front that is sewn together, this gives the effect that it is one bit of fabric tied around the head.

SUPPLIES REQUIRED

-1 Ball of regular lightweight or DK yarn in the color of your choice

-4mm crochet hook

-Tapestry needle

-Scissors

BAND INSTRUCTIONS

-Ch 81 (or however many until it fits round your head, this number won't affect your pattern so don't worry if you need more or less!)

-Row 1: hdc into the second chain from the hook and into every chain to the end of the row now chain 1 & turn your work (80).

-Row 2-8: hdc into every hdc from the previous row, ch 1 & turn (80).

-Bring the two ends of your work together and line them up on top of each other. Now using a tapestry needle and some yarn or a crochet hook attach the two ends together; by sewing or using slip stitches.

-Finish off your work and weave in any loose ends.

CENTER STRIP INSTRUCTIONS

-To begin, chain 11

-Row 1: hdc into the second chain from the hook and into every chain to the end of the row, ch 1 & turn (10).

-Row 2-8: hdc into each hdc of the row, ch 1 & turn your work.

-Finish off making sure to leave a long tail to help with sewing in the next step.

-Taking a tapestry needle along with the tail from the strip, wrap the strip around where you sewed the main headband together, this is to hide the seam! Now sew the strip together as its wrapped tightly round the headband, this is to give it the bow or turban look.

-Finish off and weave in any loose yarn you may have and your work is done. One very stylish bow or turban headband!

LACE INFINITY SCARF PATTERN

Scarves are very popular among beginners because they are easy to complete with basic crotchet techniques. Scarves are also very useful in the winter!

This pattern takes advantage of the most basic crochet technique, the chain! Now you may be thinking how can just using a chain make a scarf? Well actually it's quite easy and it looks very pretty as well.

This particular scarf is known as an infinity scarf, which means that the two ends are sewn together to make one big circle of fabric rather than one long scarf. Of course you don't have to sew the ends together if you don't want to. You can easily leave it open and it will still look great.

This project is not a short one; especially to a complete beginner this may take you a few days to complete although the fabric builds up quickly.

SUPPLIES REQUIRED

-1 ball of yarn in the color of your choice

-4mm crochet hook

-Tapestry needle

-Scissors

-A load of spare time!

SCARF INSTRUCTIONS

-Ch 40

-Row 1: Slip stitch into the 4th chain from the hook, *chain 4 then skip 3 chains, slip stitch into the 4th* repeat *to* to the end of row, ch 4 and turn. This will give you 10 distinctive loops.

-Row 2: Slip stitch into the very first loop, *chain 4 and slip stitch into the next loop* repeat *to* the end of the row, chain 4 and turn.

-Row 3: Slip stitch into the first loop of the row, *chain 4 and slip into the next loop* repeat to the end of the row, chain 4 and turn.

-At this point, keep repeating row 3 until you have reached your desired length. Keep testing along the way to make sure you make it the right length to suit your needs. I recommend a good amount of rows is between 130 and 150 depending on how tight you crochet.

-Finish off making sure to leave a long tail for sewing.

-Now line up the two edges together and use a tapestry needle with the tail you left from finishing off to neatly sew the two ends together. You can easily skip this step if you like the way the scarf looks as it is.

There you go! You have one simple, yet pretty scarf.

CHAPTER 2: INTERMEDIATE PATTERNS

So you've worked through the beginner's patterns or skipped them completely and you're confident that you would like something a little more difficult? Well this is the section for you!

This chapter is designed to step things up a notch and make the patterns a little harder. For beginners this makes a good chapter to start trying new things and experimenting, not only with your own knowledge, but also pick up some new tricks. For those of you who are quite experienced, this chapter will hopefully provide you with a couple projects that will spark your creativity or give you a cute project to work on.

This chapter will focus on items that have slightly more technical stitches such as a half double crochet, treble crochet and some other funky stitches.

2D CROCHETED APPLE APPLIQUE PATTERN

In crochet, you can use a number of 2D shapes called appliques to enhance your work in different ways; such as sticking an applique of a star to a purse or scarf. This applique pattern is in the shape of an apple and is perfect for putting on things that go in your kitchen.

SUPPLIES REQUIRED

-4mm Crochet Hook

-Red yarn (or light green if you want a green apple)

-Green yarn

-Brown yarn

-Tapestry needle

-Scissors

APPLE BODY INSTRUCTIONS

-Start off with a magic loop (this can be found in the help section at the back of the book) and chain 2.

-Rnd 1: Put 14 dc into the loop and pull it tight, slip stitch into the first dc and chain 2 (14).

-Rnd 2: 2 dc into each dc in the round, join with the first ch; don't chain! (28).

-Rnd 3: 2 dc into next 10 dc, 1 hdc in the next dc, slip stitch into the stitch, 1 hdc into next 2 dc, slip stitch in the next dc, 1 hdc in the next dc, 2 dc in each of the next 10 dc, slip stitch into the next dc.

-Finish off and use a tapestry needle to weave in any ends left over.

STEM INSTRUCTIONS

-Chain 9, sc into the second chain from the hook, single crochet into every chain to the end of the row.

-Finish off. Leave a long tail to help sew everything together at the end.

LEAF INSTRUCTIONS

-Chain 8

-Row 1: sc in second chain from the hook, hdc in the next ch, dc in the next chain. Treble crochet in the next chain, dc in the next chain, hdc in the next chain then sc into the last chain.

-Finish off. Leave a longer tail for sewing in the end.

-Begin to sew everything together using the tails you left over. Sew the stem and the leaf together before attaching the whole thing to the main apple.

-There you go! One completed Apple.

LACE BERET

This pattern incorporates some slightly more complex stitches to create something you can feel proud about and look good wearing! This project takes approximately 2 hours; however, this can vary based on how fast you work.

SUPPLIES REQUIRED

-5mm Crochet hook

-1 Ball of lightweight yarn in the color of your choice

-1 Tapestry needle

-Scissors

BERET INSTRUCTIONS

-Ch 3 (counts and first dc throughout the pattern)

-Rnd 1: dc into 3 ch from hook, dc into the same ch 10 more times, join to first dc with a sl st, ch 3 (12)

-Rnd 2: dc into same chain as the ch 3 and ch 1, *2 dc into the next st and ch 1* repeat from * in each st left in the round, join with SL st, ch 3 (you should have 11 sets of 2)

-Rnd 3: 2 dc into first st, ch 2, skip the next st (this will be the chain spaces from the previous round), *dc in next stitch, 2 dc in next stitch, chain 2, skip the next st* repeat from *to* to the end of the round, join with a sl st, ch 3 (you should have 11 sets of 3)

-Rnd 4: *dc into the next 2 st, 2 dc into the next st, ch 2, skip the next st (this should be the ch 2 space from the previous round)* repeat from *to* to the end of the round, join with a slip stitch, ch 3 (you should have 11 sets of 4)

-Rnd 5: *dc into the next 3 st, 2 dc into the next st, ch 2, skip the next st (this should be the ch 2 space from the previous round)* repeat from *to* to the end of the round, join with a slip stitch, ch 3 (you should have 11 sets of 5)

-Rnd 6: *dc into the next 4 st, 2 dc into the next st, ch 2, skip the next st (this should be the ch 2 space from the previous round)* repeat from *to* to the end of the round, join with a slip stitch, ch 3 (you should have 11 sets of 6)

-Rnd 7: *dc into the next 5 st, 2 dc into the next st, ch 2, skip the next st (this should be the ch 2 space from the previous round)* repeat from *to* to the end of the round, join with a slip stitch, ch 3 (you should have 11 sets of 7)

-Rnd 8: *dc into the next 6 st, 2 dc into the next st, ch 2, skip the next st (this should be the ch 2 space from the previous round)* repeat from *to* to the end of the round, join with slip stitch, ch 3 (you should have 11 sets of 8)

-Rnd 9-10: repeat round 8, at the end of round 10, ch 2 instead of 3

-Rnd 11: sc into each st around, join with a SL st, ch 2

-Rnd 12: *skip the next st, sc into the next st* repeat all the way around, join with a SL st and ch 2.

-(Note: Test the beret, if it is too large, repeat round 12 again. If it is too small, redo round 12 but loosen up your stitches)

-Rnd 13-16: sc in each st around, join with a SL st and ch 2

-Finish off and use a tapestry needle to tidy up and weave in in loose ends.

This Beret's makes excellent last minute present idea or just as a funky hat for you that looks great no matter the weather!

MOUSTACHE PILLOW

Like the previous pattern, this is a fantastic project for those that would like a more challenging pattern!

This crochet pattern is designed and made to roughly fit an 18 inch by 18 inch pillow. This is the perfect project to accompany the growing moustache fad that seems to be gaining popularity. The pattern itself is fairly simple, but can take a few days to finish.

This pattern finishes by permanently sewing the pillow inside of the pillow case. You can wash the entire pillow but if it is your preference you may want to finish your pillow differently than. For example you can add buttons or a zipper so that you can get the pillow out of the mustache pillow case.

This pattern is worked by creating a number of rectangles in each color before sewing together to create two large panels. In total you will need 32 rectangles, 16 in white and 16 in black. The numbers in brackets at the end of each row indicate the number of stitches you should have in that row.

SUPPLIES REQUIRED

- 1 ball of Black Yarn

- 2 balls of White Yarn

- A 4mm Crochet Hook

- 1 Tapestry needle

- 1 18" by 18" Pillow Pad

- Scissors

- A lot of Patience!

PILLOW CASE INSTRUCTIONS

-Beginning with the white yarn and a 4mm crochet hook:

-Ch 16

-**Row 1**: half double crochet into the second chain from hook, then into each ch to the end of the row, ch 2 and turn (15)

-**Row 2**: hdc into each hdc until you reach the end of the row, chain 2 and turn (15)

-**Row 3-10:** Repeat row 2 (15)

-Finish off leaving a long tail, this assists with assembly later

-Make 15 more of the white panels

Next, with the Black yarn and a 4mm crochet hook:

-Ch 16

-**Row 1:** hdc into the second chain from hook, then into each ch to the end of the row, ch 2 and turn (15)

-**Row 2:** hdc into each hdc until you get to the end of the row, chain 2 and turn your work (15)

-**Row 3-10:** Repeat row 2 (15)

-Finish off leaving a long tail, this assists with assembly later

-Make 15 more of the Black panels

MOUSTACHE INSTRUCTIONS

Using Black yarn and a 4 mm crochet hook:

-Ch 5

-SC into second ch from hook,

-HDC into next ch,

-DC into the next ch,

-2 HDC in the last ch, place a stitch marker in the chain

-Do not finish off!

-Now ch 6 from your current point

-SL st into the second ch from hook,

-SL st into the next 2 chains,

-SC into the next ch,

-2 HDC in the last available ch (Note: the last ch may be difficult to see due to its position)

-You will now attach the extension you just made by working back down the original ch 5 you did in the beginning

-DC into the first ch marked by the stitch marker (There tends to be a gap formed by doing this, don't worry that's supposed to happen!)

-HDC into the next ch

-SC into the next ch

-SL ST into the last ch and finish off.

-Repeat to create the other half of the moustache the sew the two halves together

-You will need 16 Moustaches in total

ASSEMBLY INSTRUCTIONS

You will be forming a 4x4 grid using the panels, alternating the colors (e.g. black then white) to create something that looks like a checkerboard.

-Sew the moustache appliques to the Centre of the white panels and begin by sewing each of the panels together in a row.

-Do this for each of the rows until you end up with 4 long strips, now sew each of the strips together.

-You should now have one large panel.

-Repeat this process to form the other panel.

-To sew the panels together to create a pillow case, lay both panels together and begin sewing through both panels around 3 sides of the panels, now turn your pillow case right side out and insert the pillow pad into the case. Now sew along the remaining side to close the case.

-If you are using an alternate method such as adding a zipper and buttons, go ahead and do that now in replacement of the last step.

And there you go, one completed moustache pillow!

THICK WINTER HEADBAND

Now I know you're thinking, a headband? In winter? Yes I know it sounds a little weird but this headband is designed to be stylish and warm without leaving you with hat hair! This pattern contains a simple yet beautiful flower pattern that is used to decorate the headband.

For this pattern you will need to use very chunky yarn otherwise the pattern will not work. You can super bulky yarn or if that isn't readily available you can use 2-3 strands of other yarn all together to get the same thickness.

SUPPLIES REQUIRED

-Super chunky yarn in the color of your choice
-7-8mm crochet hook
-Tapestry needle
-Scissors

HEADBAND INSTRUCTIONS

-Ch 11

-Row 1: Single crochet into each chain, chain 1 and turn (10).

-Row 2: Single crochet in the back loop of the stitches to the end of the row, chain 1 and turn (10).

-Row 3-22 (or however many it takes to fit your head, the number of rows does not matter in this pattern): Single crochet into the back loops only as in row 2 till you reach the end of the row, chain 1 and turn (10).

-Finish off as usual and make sure to leave a long enough tail to sew the whole thing together.

-Take a tapestry needle and line the two edges of the headband up so they are even, neatly sew them together through the stitches. At this point it is a good idea to sew your choice of decoration (if you are using one that is) over the seam this creates; this way it hides it completely.

Next is a simple pattern for a traditional Christmas flower called a Poinsettia. It is very common in stores in the holiday season and has a very distinctive look with big pointy star like leaves and a beautiful bright red color.

POINSETTIA FLOWER INSTRUCTIONS

Using a magic loop:

-Rnd 1: * do 2 single crochets and a chain 2* repeat this pattern six times within the loop, after the last set slip stitch st into the first sc, then tighten up the loop.

-Rnd 2: For this round you will be working into the chain 2 spaces from the first round. Work these stitches into every one of the chain 2 spaces: *sc, dc, tr, dc, sc*. This creates one petal, repeat this process all the way around; this should leave you with 6 petals, finish off and weave in any loose ends.

-At this point you can leave the flower exactly as it is or you may choose to decorate it either with some sparkly jewels or even some big patterned buttons. If you choose to add decorations make sure to attach them before attaching the whole flower to the headband.

CHAPTER 3: ADVANCED PATTERNS

You've breezed through the beginners patterns and conquered the intermediate chapter and now you're looking for a challenge? Well this chapter is what you're looking for. This chapter offers projects that are more challenging, especially if you have not been crocheting for very long. The patterns in this chapter are either very complex with a number of different stitches per row and are very long and in depth projects.

BABY BOOTIES

These little baby slippers or boots make great little last minute presents. This project can easily be completed within a few hours and you are free to customize this to your hearts content!

This pattern uses a size 3.5 or a 4mm hook to make boots suitable for a 0-6 month old baby. However, you can alter this size by simply changing the hook size and yarn type and not changing the pattern at all. For example you can switch out the regular yarn for super bulky yarn and a 8mm hook and get boots big enough for a 4-6 year old child.

SUPPLIES REQUIRED

-Yarn of your choice, we recommend lightweight yarn

-3.5 or 4mm crochet hook depending on the size you want

-Tapestry needle

-Scissors

BOOTIES INSTRUCTIONS

-Ch 9

-Rnd 1: Put 2 double crochets in the 3rd chain from the hook, dc again into next 5 chains, 6 dc into the last ch of the row, turn your work so you can work along the opposite side of the chain, dc into the next 5 ch, 3 dc in the last chain then finally sl st into the top of the first chain, ch 2 (22)

-Rnd 2: hdc into the same space as the slip stitch from the first round, 2 hdc into each of the next 2 stitches, hdc into the next 5 stitches, 2 hdc in each of the next 6 stitches, hdc into the next 5 stitches, 2 hdc in each of next 3 stitches and finally join with a slip stitch and chain 2 (34)

-Rnd 3: hdc into the back loop of each stitch in the row, this is to mold the shape of the sole, join with a slip stitch and chain 2 (34)

-Rnd 4: hdc into the next 8 stitches, dc2tog 8 times, hdc in next 9 stitches, join with a slip stitch and chain 2 (26)

-Rnd 5: hdc in next 8 stitches, dc2tog 4 times, hdc into the next 9 stitches, join with a slip stitch and chain 2 (22)

-Rnd 6: hdc in next 8 stitches, dc2tog 2 times, hdc in the next 9 stitches, join with a slip stitch and chain 2 (20)

-Rnd 7-8: hdc into each stitch in the round, join with a slip stitch and chain 1 (20)

-Rnd 9: single crochet into each stitch in the round to give a nice border to your work (20)

-If you want the booties to be longer, repeat round 9 as many times as you would like before ending.

-Fasten off and weave in loose ends.

And there you go! One adorable pair of baby booties! These shoes have a tendency to slide on wood or tiled floors. To fix this you can sew felt pads or use hot glue to make dots on the bottoms of the slippers to make them grip floors better.

CROCHETED CAT DOORSTOP/ORNAMENT

The principles of this pattern are incredibly basic, but the number of components and the scale of this project can make it a challenge.

This pattern is very similar to amigurumi which is a crocheting technique that is covered later on in this guide. If you are unfamiliar with amigurumi please see the chapter 4, for more information.

SUPPLIES REQUIRED

- 4mm crochet hook

- 1 ball of DK yarn in the main color of the cat (you will have lots left over)

- Small amount of black yarn

- Small amount of white yarn

- Small amount of pink yarn

- Small amount of a random color for the collar

- 1 pipe cleaner

- 1 small bell

- 1 small plastic sandwich bag

- 1 small handful of rice/lentils/something dry you don't mind using

- Toy filler

- 2 large google eyes

-You may want to use a stitch marker for this pattern due to each round being continuous.

HEAD INSTRUCTIONS

Using a magic loop:

-Rnd 1: Put 6 sc into the loop and tighten (6)

-Rnd 2: Now do 2 sc into each sc of the previous round (12)

-Rnd 3: *1 sc into the first sc, 2 sc into the next sc* repeat *to* till you reach the end of the round (18)

-Rnd 4: Do 1 sc into each stitch in the round (18)

-Rnd 5: *1 sc into the next 2 stitches, 2 sc in the next stitch* repeat *to* to finish the round (24)

-Rnd 6: Put 1 sc into every stitch in the round (24)

-Rnd 7: *1 sc into the next 3 sc, 2 sc into the follow sc* repeat *to* to complete the round (30)

-Rnd 7: Put 1 sc into every stitch in the round (30)

-Rnd 8: *1 sc into the next 4 stitches, 2 sc into the next stitch* repeat *to* to complete the round (36)

Rnd 9: Put 1 sc into every stitch in the round (36)

-Rnd 10: *1 sc into the next 5 stitches, 2 sc in the next stitch* repeat *to* to complete the round (42)

-Rnd 11: Put 1 sc into every stitch in the round (42)

-Rnd 12: *1 sc into the next 6 stitches, 2 sc into the next stitch* repeat *to* to complete the round (48)

-Rnd 13-16: Put 1 sc into every stitch in the round (48)

-Rnd 17: *1 sc into the next 6 stitches, decrease* repeat *to* to complete the round (42)

-Rnd 18: Put 1 sc into every stitch in the round (42)

-Rnd 19: *1 sc into the next 5 stitches, decrease* repeat *to* to complete the round (36)

-Rnd 20: Put 1 sc into every stitch in the round (36)

-Rnd 21: *1 sc into the next 4 stitches, decrease* repeat *to* to complete the round (30)

-Rnd 22: Put 1 sc into every stitch in the round (30)

-Start stuffing and shaping the head now.

-Rnd 23: *1 sc into the next 3 stitches, decrease* repeat *to* to complete the round (24)

-Rnd 24: *1 sc into the next 2 stitches, decrease* repeat *to* to complete the round (18)

-Rnd 25: *1 sc in the next stitch, decrease* repeat *to* to complete the round (12)

-Rnd 26: decrease in every stitch (6)

-Finish off and insert a tapestry needle onto the remaining yarn, use this to sew the remaining hole shut and weave in any loose bits.

BODY INSTRUCTIONS

Using a magic loop:

-Rnd 1: Put 6 sc into the loop and tighten (6)

-Rnd 2: Now do 2 sc into each sc of the previous round (12)

-Rnd 3: *1 sc into the first sc, 2 sc into the next sc* repeat *to* till you reach the end of the round (18)

-Rnd 4: *1 sc into the next 2 stitches, 2 sc in the next stitch* repeat *to* to finish the round (24)

-Rnd 5: *1 sc into the next 3 stitches, 2 sc in the next stitch* repeat *to* to finish the round (30)

-Rnd 6: *1 sc into the next 4 stitches, 2 sc in the next stitch* repeat *to* to finish the round (36)

-Rnd 7: *1 sc into the next 5 stitches, 2 sc in the next stitch* repeat *to* to finish the round (42)

-Rnd 8: *1 sc into the next 6 stitches, 2 sc in the next stitch* repeat *to* to finish the round (48)

-Rnd 9: *1 sc into the next 7 stitches, 2 sc in the next stitch* repeat *to* to finish the round (54)

-Rnd 10-12: Put 1 sc into every stitch in the round (54)

-Rnd 13: *1 sc in the next 7 sc then decrease* repeat to finish the round (48)

-Rnd 14: Put 1 sc into every stitch in the round (48)

-Rnd 15: *1 sc in the next 6 sc then decrease* repeat to finish the round (42)

-Rnd 16: Put 1 sc into every stitch in the round (42)

-Rnd 17: *1 sc in the next 5 sc then decrease* repeat to finish the round (36)

-Rnd 18: Put 1 sc into every stitch in the round (36)

-Rnd 19: *1 sc in the next 4 sc then decrease* repeat to finish the round (30)

-Rnd 20: Put 1 sc into every stitch in the round (30)

-At this point, fill a small plastic sandwich bag or a small container with the weight of your choice. If this project is going to be used as a doorstop you may want to put some stones or an actual weight inside. If not using as doorstop then you can use something lighter such as sand, rice or lentils. Insert your weight into the cavity.

-Rnd 21: *1 sc in the next 3 sc then decrease* repeat to finish the round (24)

-Rnd 22: Put 1 sc into every stitch in the round (24)

-Begin stuff the body cavity with the toy filler around the weight making sure to shape the cat as you go.

-Rnd 23: *1 sc in the next 2 sc then decrease* repeat to finish the round (18)

-Rnd 24-26: Put 1 sc into every stitch in the round (18)

-Once finished, complete stuffing the body cavity and ensure it is in a shape you like before moving on to assembly.

ASSEMBLY INSTRUCTIONS

Begin by lining up everything to ensure everything fits right. You can use sewing pins to hold everything in place while you sew. Now taking a tapestry needle and some yarn of the same color as the cat's body, begin to neatly stitch around the base of the neck to connect the head and body together. Keep your stitches as neat and small as possible, use the single crochets as a guide for where to stitch.

EARS INSTRUCTIONS (MAKE 2 INNER EARS AND 2 OUTER EARS)

Outer Ear

Using a magic loop:

-Rnd 1: Put 6 sc and then tighten up the loop (6)

-Rnd 2: *1 sc into the next 2 stitches, 2 sc in the next stitch* repeat *to* to finish the round (8)

-Rnd 3: *1 sc into the next 3 stitches, 2 sc in the next stitch* repeat *to* to finish the round (10)

-Rnd 4: **1 sc into the next 4 stitches, 2 sc in the next stitch* repeat *to* to finish the round (12)

-Rnd 5: *1 sc into the next 2 stitches, 2 sc in the next stitch* repeat *to* to finish the round (16)

-Rnd 6: *1 sc into the next 3 stitches, 2 sc in the next stitch* repeat *to* to finish the round (20)

-Rnd 7: *1 sc into the next 4 stitches, 2 sc in the next stitch* repeat *to* to finish the round (24)

-Rnd 8-9: sc into every stitch in the round (24)

-Finish off making sure to leave a long tail for attaching the ears to the head.

Inner Ear (in pink)

-Chain 7

-Row 1: hdc2tog into the first 2 chains, hdc in the next 2 ch, hdc2tog in the last 2 ch, ch 1 and turn (4)

-Row 2: hdc2tog in first 2 stitches, hdc2tog in last 2 stitches, ch 1 and turn (2)

-Row 3: hdc2tog twice, chain 2 (1)

-Finish off leaving enough yarn for sewing everything together.

-Sew the inner and outer ear bits together to form the ears.

TAIL INSTRUCTIONS

In a magic loop:

-Rnd 1: Do 6 sc and then tighten up the loop.

-Rnd 2: Do 1 sc into each sc in the round (6).

-Repeat round 2 until the tail is as long as you want it, we went for 7 inches.

-Finish off leaving a long tail.

-Now taking your pipe cleaners fold them in half and insert them into the tail.

-Bend the tail into the shape you want your tail to be.

-Use a tapestry needle to attach the tail.

-Run a few stitches along where the tail touches the back of the cat for more support.

-Neaten everything up and you're done!

It took a while, but now you have your very own doorstopper shaped like a cat! From here you can adjust this pattern to make the cat look however you like. You can change the colors or add more spots and stripes, it's up to you!

BABY BLANKET

Crocheted blankets of any kind are notorious for being ongoing and boring projects and as such become more difficult to complete. This pattern is designed to be worked in 3 sections that you will repeat again and again to create your blanket. This makes the project easier to do as you can break your work down into smaller easier sections. You can pick whatever colors you would like for this particular project.

Although this project does take quite a bit of time to do, it makes a fantastic present for any occasion or even to make for yourself if you have a buddle of joy on the way!

SUPPLIES REQUIRED

-3 balls of lightweight yarn in various colors

-A 4mm crochet hook

-Tapestry needle

-Scissors

-Patience!

BLANKET INSTRUCTIONS

Throughout this pattern, your first color or section will be known as A, your second color or section will be known as B and the last color or section will be known as C.

-Ch 91 with A

-Row 1: hdc into second ch from hook, hdc into each st to end of row, ch 2, turn (90)

-Row 2: hdc into each st to end of row, Attach B with a SL st, ch 3 and turn (90)

-Row 3: dc into same space as the ch 3 (This counts as first V Stitch),* miss next 2 hdc, 1 dc, ch 1, 1 dc into same st*, repeat from * to * until end of row, Attach C with a SL st, ch 3 and turn (You should have 30 V's)

-Row 4: 2 dc into first V Stitch (ch 3 counts as first), 3 dc into each V Stitch until end of row, attach A with a SL st, ch 2 and turn (90)

-Row 5: hdc into the second chain from the hook, hdc into each stitch to end of row, ch 2 and turn (90)

-Row 6: hdc into each stitch to the end of the row, Attach B with a slip stitch, ch 3 and turn (90)

-Row 7: dc into same space as the ch 3 you did,* miss the next 2 hdc and then do 1 dc, ch 1, 1 dc into same st*, repeat from * to * until end of row, Attach C with a slip stitch, ch 3 and turn.

-Row 8: 2 dc into the first V Stitch and then 3 dc into each V Stitch until the end of row; attach A with a slip stitch, ch 2 and turn (90)

-Row 9: hdc into second chain from the hook, hdc into each stitch to the end of the row, ch 2, turn (90)

-Row 10: hdc into each stitch to the end of the row, Attach B with a slip stitch, ch 3 and turn (90)

-Row 11: dc into the same space as the ch 3 you did,* miss the next 2 hdc, then 1 dc, ch 1, 1 dc into same st*, repeat from * to * until end of row, Attach C with a slip stitch, ch 3 and turn (You should have 30 V stitches)

-Row 12: 2 dc into your first V Stitch, put 3 dc into each V Stitch until end of row, now attach A with a slip stitch, ch 2 and turn your work (90)

-Repeat rows 8-12 until the blanket is the length you would like it to be.

-Now using the first color you used (A), begin to double crochet all the way around the blanket, this gives a nice border to your work and neatens up everything.

-Note: When adding the border, add 3 extra dc on the corners to stop the blankets edges from curling up

-Fasten off.

Now comes the "fun part"

-Taking a tapestry needle, begin weaving in and trimming off loose ends. This can take a while depending on the size of the blanket you make so put on some music or your favorite TV show and get to work!

And there you go! One adorable baby blanket!

CHAPTER 4: AMIGURUMI

WHAT IS AMIGURUMI?

Amigurumi is a special type of crochet that is used in crocheted toy making. Amigurumi refers the special process used to make animals or objects with anthropomorphic features such as eyes.

WHERE DID AMIGURUMI ORIGINATE?

Amigurumi first made its appearance in the early 2000 in Japan. It became popular due to the bright colors and funky animals and shapes you can create. News of amigurumi spread and soon could be found in different variations and forms around the world, as well as an extensive amount of patterns and tutorials littering the internet.

HOW IS AMIGURUMI DIFFERENT FROM REGULAR CROCHET?

Amigurumi and regular crochet are very similar. The way amigurumi is different from a simple panel of fabric is where you put your stitches and how you start your work. Amigurumi usually exclusively uses single crochet as well as increasing and decreasing stitches. It is done this way because of the tightness of the stitches which works well for holding filling.

Instead of starting your work with a chain like you would normally, almost all modern amigurumi patterns use a magic loop. This starting method leaves no holes in your work and it gives your work a very clean and polished look.

Another distinctive characteristic of amigurumi is that you will rarely turn your work or join at any point. To complete this you are required to work in continuous rounds without joining. This gives the finished product a very clean look with no seams.

WILL I NEED ANY SPECIAL TOOLS TO DO AMIGURUMI?

Absolutely not! You can use all your regular tools such as crochet hooks and yarn, the only extra thing you need when making toys is filling. For example for a cuddly toy you can use pillow stuffing or toy stuffing. If your project is cube shape then you can use a small box or some cardboard to fill your item with to give it nice crisp edges.

BASIC AMIGURUMI BALL PATTERN

This is a very simple pattern that allows you to get the feel of how amigurumi works; we will be working in rounds (working in a circle) and will only be using single crochet for this pattern.

This is a very versatile object as the completed object allows you to create whatever you would like out of it. You may choose to make it in bright yellow and then sew a cute emoticon face to it or you may choose to fill it with rice or some other kind of weight to make a usable ball. The choice is up to you.

The finished ball should fit nicely in an adults hand; however you can expand or shrink the size of the ball simply by using a bigger or smaller hook.

This pattern requires the use of a continuous round so you will not be joining or turning your work at any point. Due to the nature of this pattern you may want to use stitch markers to mark out where the beginning of your rounds are, otherwise your stitches can be tricky to see.

SUPPLIES REQUIRED

-1 ball of DK (lightweight) yarn in the color of your choice

-A 4mm crochet hook

-Stitch markers

-Tapestry needle

-Scissors

-Your choice of filling for the ball

INSTRUCTIONS

To begin, make a magic loop

-Rnd 1: Put 6 sc into the ring, tighten up the loop to close the hole and continue (6)

-Rnd 2: 2 sc into each of the sc in the ring (12)

-Rnd 3: *sc into the next sc, 2 sc into the next sc* repeat *to* around (18)

-Rnd 4: *sc into the next 2 sc, 2 sc into the next sc* repeat *to* around (24)

-Rnd 5: *sc into the next 3 sc, 2 sc into the next sc* repeat *to* around (30)

-Rnd 6: *sc into the next 4 sc, 2 sc into the next sc* repeat *to* around (36)

-Rnd 7: *sc into the next 5 sc, 2 sc into the next sc* repeat *to* around (42)

-Rnd 8-13: sc in each stitch around (42)

-Rnd 14:* sc into the next 5 sc, decrease in next 2 sc* repeat around (36)

-Rnd 15: *sc into the next 4 sc, decrease in next 2 sc* repeat around (30)

-Rnd 16: *sc into the next 3 sc, decrease in next 2 sc* repeat around (24)

-At this point you may begin to fill the ball with the filling of your choice. If using a weight such as rice you may want to put it in a small bag first so it doesn't work its way through your stitches and fall out. If stuffing with toy filling, make sure to pack it in tight to give the ball structure.

-Rnd 17: *sc into the next 2 sc, decrease in next 2 sc* repeat around (18)

-Rnd 18: *sc in next sc, dec in next 2 sc* repeat around (12)

-Rnd 19: dec in next 2 sc around (6)

-Finish off and use a tapestry needle to sew in any loose ends and you're done!

EASY AMIGURUMI CHICK

Now that you have mastered the basics of amigurumi you can move on to creating an actual animal! The principle from the last pattern is still the same; you are just increasing and decreasing in different locations to create some shape. This is still a very easy beginner level and can easily be done in about an hour.

SUPPLIES REQUIRED

-A small amount of lightweight yellow yarn

-4mm crochet hook

-Tapestry needle

-Toy filler

-Scissors

-A little orange and white yarn

This pattern is worked in continuous rounds so make sure to use a stitch marker to keep track of where your rows are.

BODY INSTRUCTIONS

-Start off with a magic loop

-Rnd 1: Put 6 sc into the magic loop and then tighten it (6)

-Rnd 2: Put 2 sc into each of the sc around (12)

-Rnd 3: *1 sc into the next sc, 2 sc in the next sc* Repeat *to* around (18)

-Rnd 4: *1 sc into the next 2 sc, 2 sc in the next sc* Repeat *to* around (24)

-Rnd 5: *1 sc into the next 3 sc, 2 sc in the next sc* Repeat *to* around (30)

-Rnd 6-16: 1 sc into each sc around (30)

-Rnd 17: *1 sc into the next 3 sc, sc2tog* repeat *to* around (24)

-Rnd 18: *1 sc in the next 2 sc, sc2tog* Repeat *to* around (18)

-Rnd 19: *1 sc in the next sc, sc2tog* Repeat *to* around (12)

-Stuff the open cavity at this point with toy filler.

-Rnd 20: sc2tog around this round to close the hole that's left.

-Finish off and weave in any loose ends.

-Using a tapestry needle and bits of orange and white yarn, sew in the details such as the beak and little tuft of fluff on the top of the chicks head.

WINGS & TAIL INSTRUCTIONS

Make 3

-In a magic loop,

-**Rnd 1:** 6 sc, tighten the loop (6)

-**Rnd 2:** 2 sc in each sc (12)

-**Rnd 3-5:** 1 sc in each sc (12)

-Finish off leaving a long tail for sewing

-The feet are made from 1 orange pipe cleaner, I simply folded it into little V shapes and split it in half to form the feet, to attach them I used excess yarn from sewing the tail on to sew the feet in place but feel free to use glue if you're more comfortable with that.

And there you go! One easy adorable little chick! You can use the same body pattern to make a number of different animals.

CHAPTER 5: TIPS & TRICKS

This chapter is designed to answer any questions you may have had while working the patterns in this book. If there is a term or abbreviation you don't understand it will be here as well as a conversion chart for hook sizes. There is also a tutorial for how to do a magic loop which is a frequent starting method throughout this book.

HOOK CONVERSION CHART

All of the hook sizes in this book are listed in millimeters. This chart will show give you the conversion from millimeters to standard sizing.

Metric Sizing – Hook Size In mm	US Standard Sizing
2.0	-
2.25	1/B
2.5	-
2.75	C
3.0	-
3.25	D
3.5	4/E
3.75	F
4.0	6/G
4.5	7
5.0	8/H
5.5	9/I
6.0	10/J
6.5	10.5/K
7.0	-
8.0	11/L
9.0	13/M
10.0	15/N

STITCH ABBREVIATIONS

All of the patterns in this book are written using US crochet terms. However, all of the terms used are in their shortened or abbreviated form. This table shows the crochet abbreviations and their corresponding meaning.

Crochet Terminology	Abbreviation
Slip Stitch	SS or Sl St
Chain	Ch
Single Crochet	Sc
Single Crochet Two Together	sc2tog
Increasing	Inc.
Decreasing	Dec
Back Loop Only	BLO
Double Crochet	Dc
Half Double Crochet	Hdc
Repeat	Rep
Millimeter	Mm
Alternate	Alt
Treble Crochet	Tr
**	Repeat as instructed
Continue	Cont.

HOW TO MAKE A MAGIC LOOP

A magic loop is a technique used to start off crochet projects that are round. It is commonly used in amigurumi as well as in making hats. Following is a basic tutorial on how to do a magic loop.

Begin by wrapping the yarn once around two fingers. The tail of your yarn should be furthest from you and the other end of the yarn connected to the ball should be closest to you.

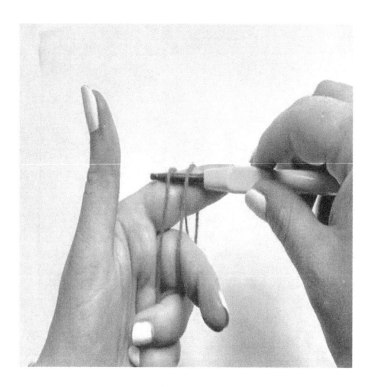

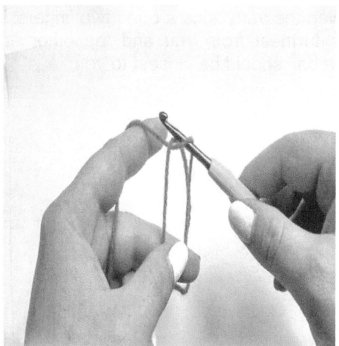

Hold on to the tail tight for the next part, you should clearly see two bits of yarn over your fingers. Now take your crochet hook and put it under the first loop and hook on to the second.

Now pull it through the first loop and using the longer bit of yarn, chain 2.

You are now free to put as many stitches as you need in this loop. For demonstration purposes 8 single crochets have been used here. Once complete, pull on the tail to close up the loop.

And there you go one basic magic loop. These are fantastic to use if you don't want any large holes in your work and to give round projects or amigurumi a nice clean finish.